For as he thinketh in his heart, so is he...
Proverbs 23:7

Written by
Karen Porter and Dr. Martha Watts

Illustrated by
Karen Porter

EMOTION MANDALAS

Try some of these shapes in your mandala or find new doodles that express the way you feel.

 Petals

 Lines

 Triangles

 Circles with dots

 Triangles and dots

 Long petals

 Curved and pointy petals

 Swirls and spirals

 Tear drops within teardrops

 Triangles within triangles with lines

 Curved and pointy petals with teardrops inside or long petals.

Confident

To feel like you can do anything well.

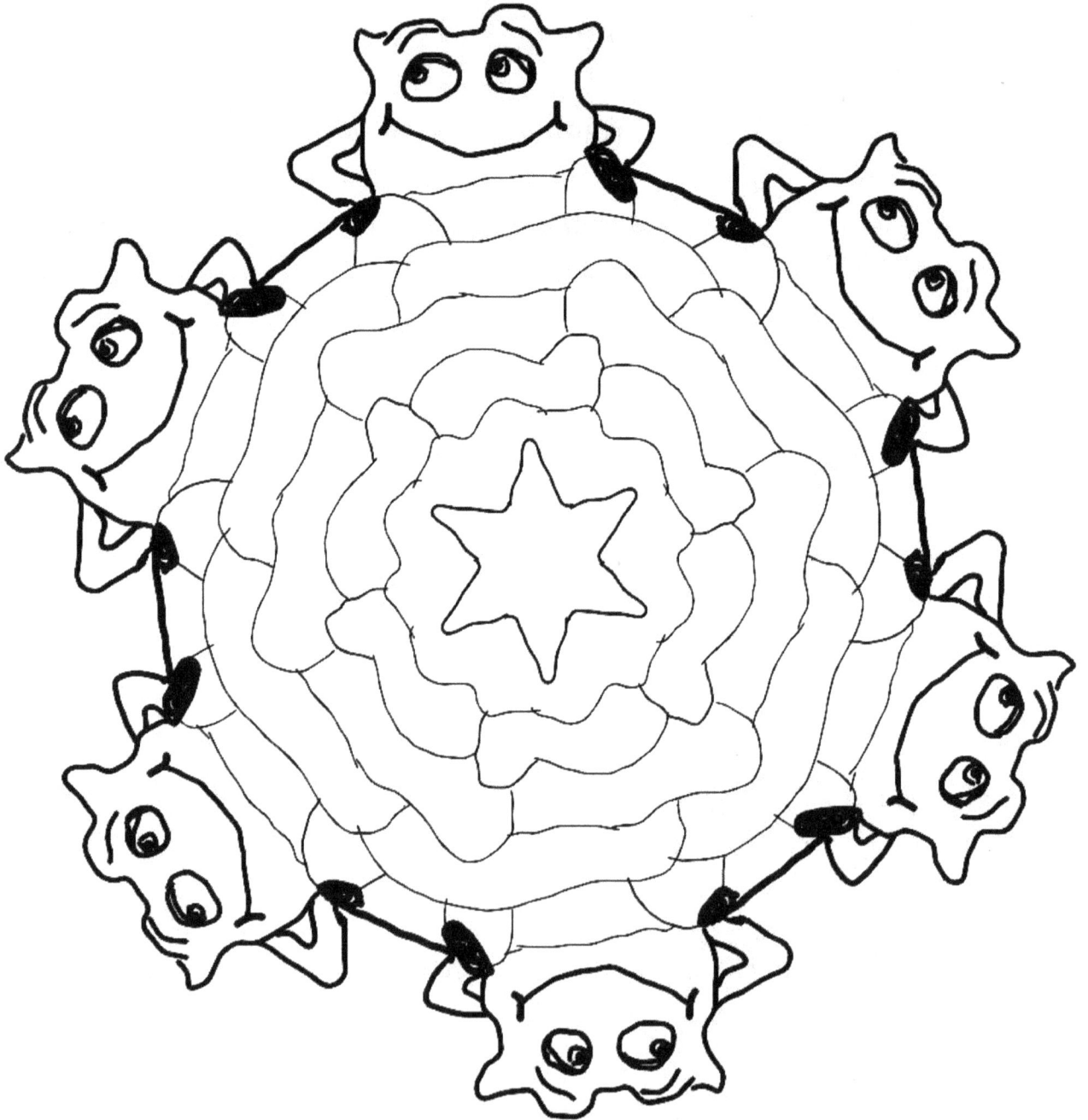

Fill this mandala with colors that express your experience of confidence.

Confident

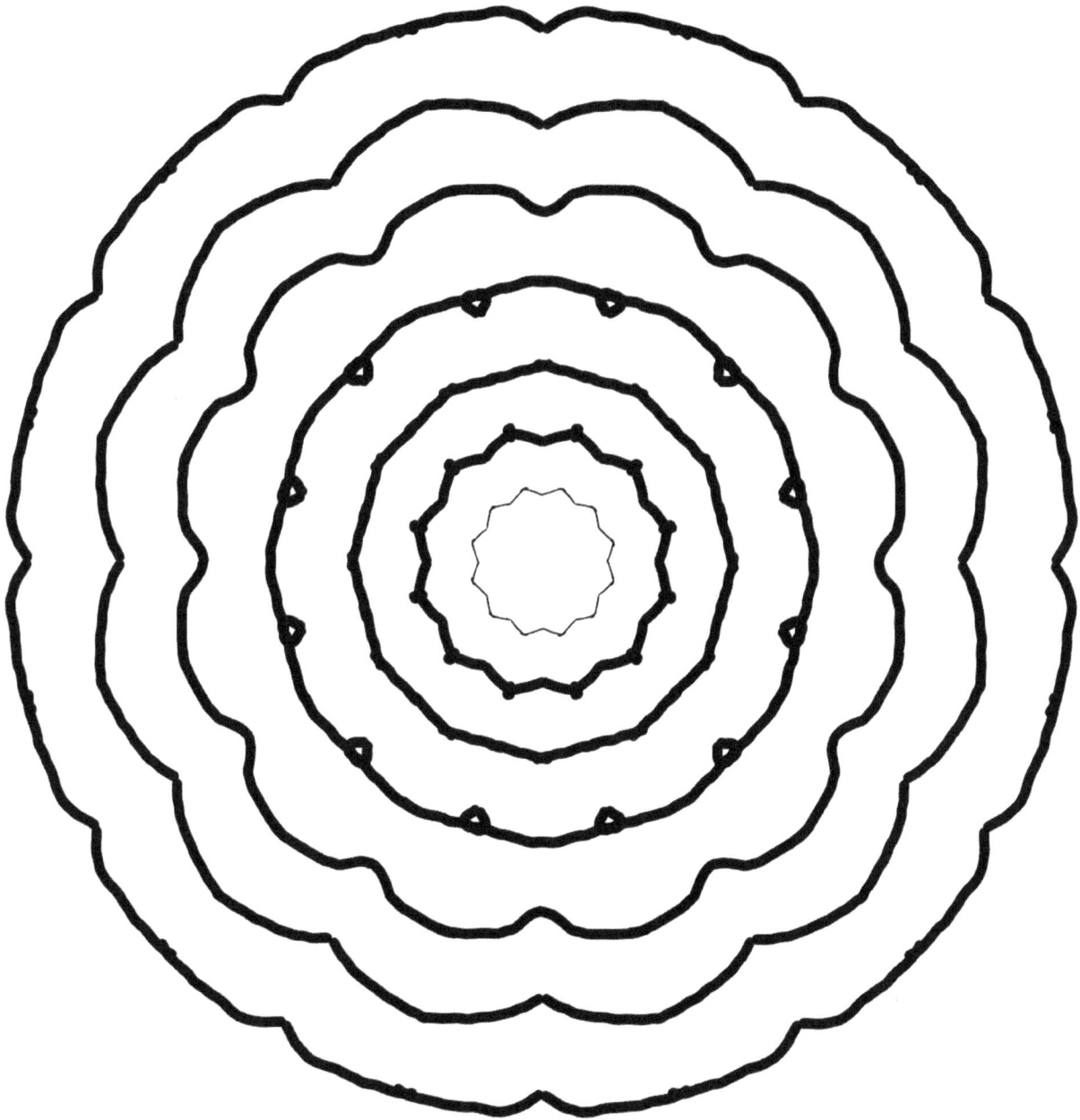

Add lines, shapes, and colors to this mandala so it
expresses your experience of confidence.

Fear

To feel like something can hurt you.

Fill this mandala with colors that express your experience of fear.

Fear

To feel like something can hurt you.

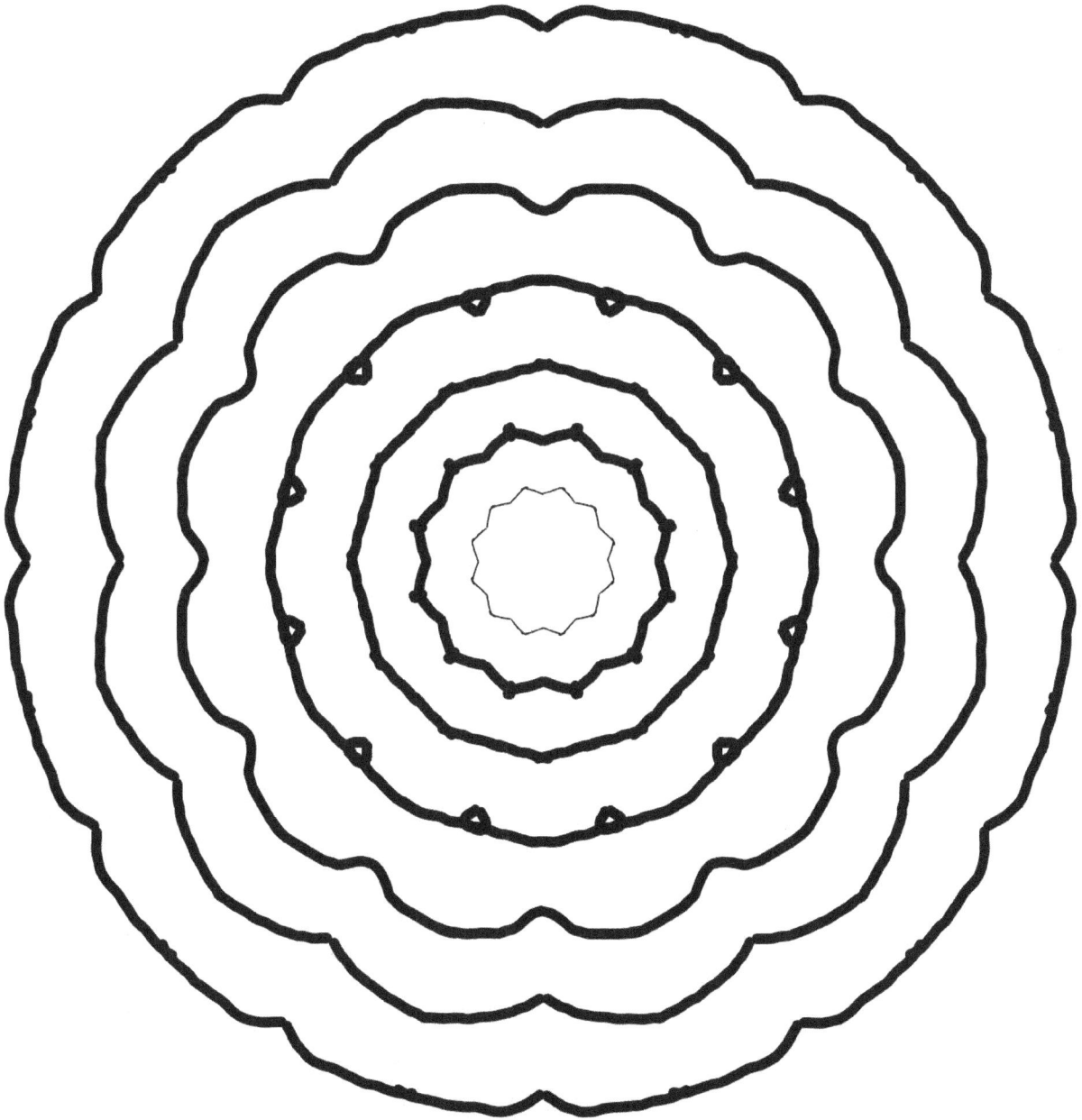

Add lines, shapes, and colors to this mandala so it
expresses your experience of fear.

Excited

To feel everything is awesome.

Fill this mandala with colors that express
your experience of excitement.

Excited

To feel everything is awesome.

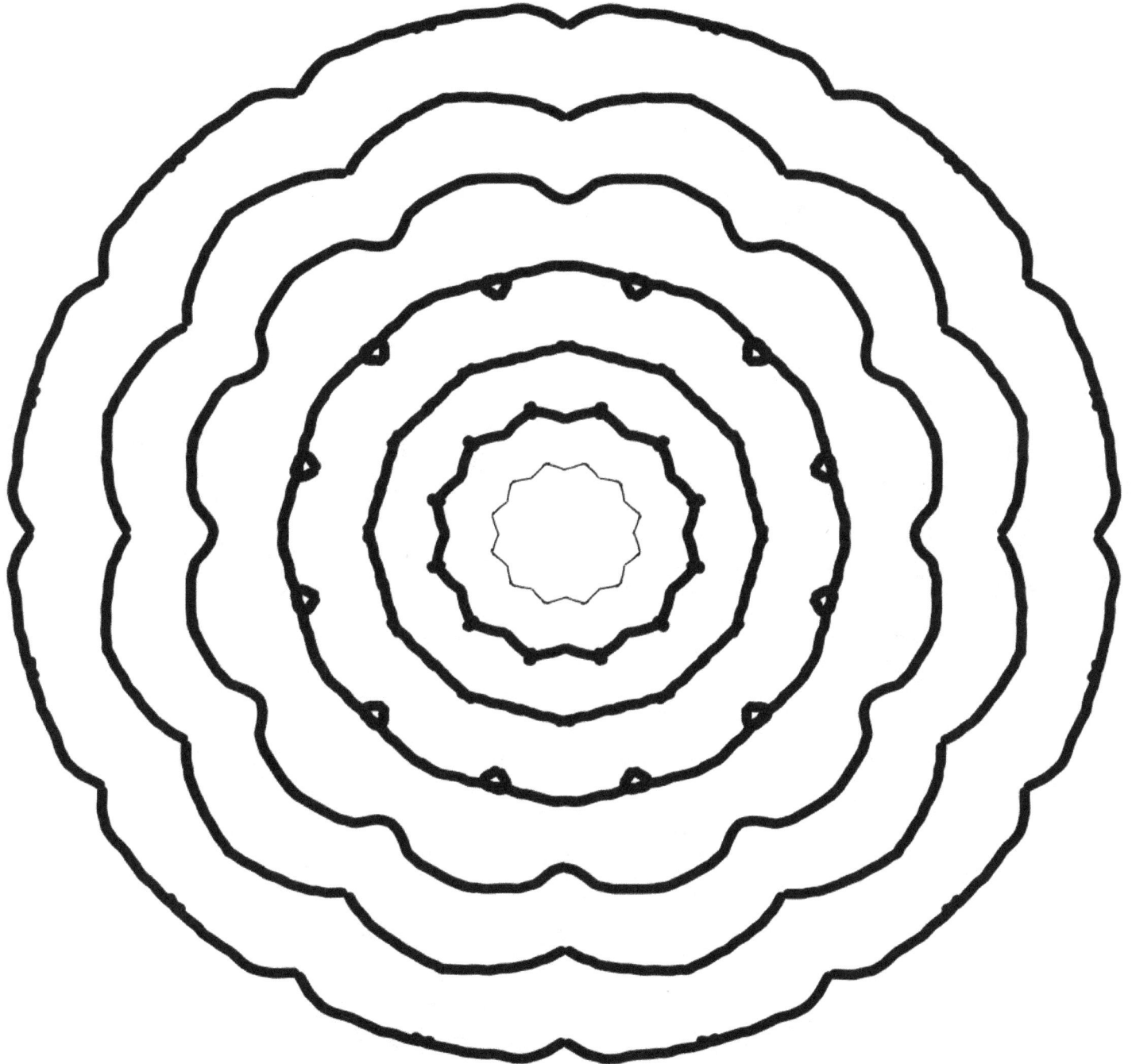

Add lines, shapes, and colors to this mandala so it
expresses your experience of excitement.

Angry

To feel like somebody did something
wrong to you.

Fill this mandala with colors that express
your experience of anger.

Angry

To feel like somebody did something
wrong to you.

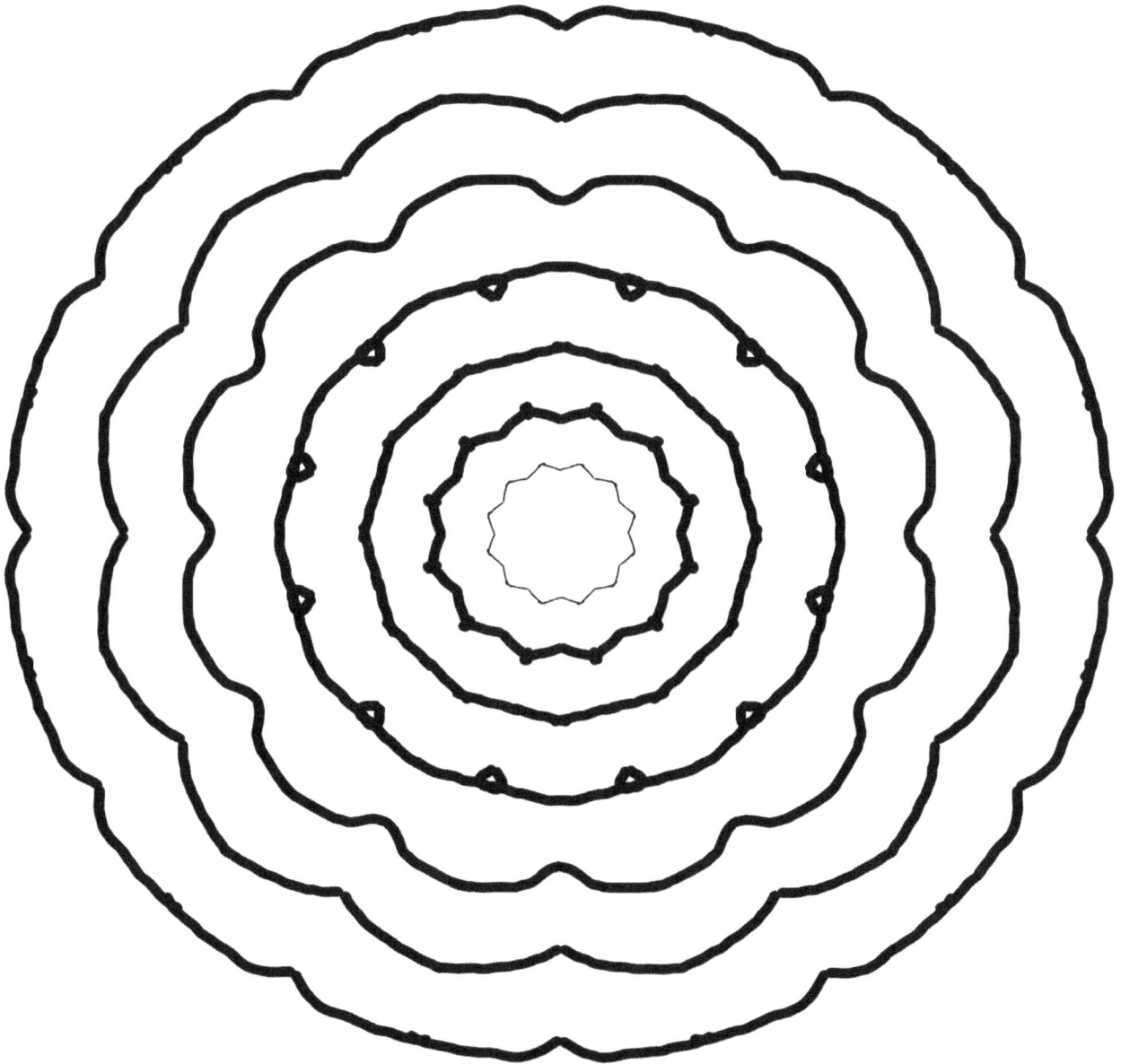

Add lines, shapes, and colors to this mandala so it
expresses your experience of anger.

Happy

To feel glad like you want to smile.

Fill this mandala with colors that express
your experience of happiness.

Happy

To feel glad like you want to smile.

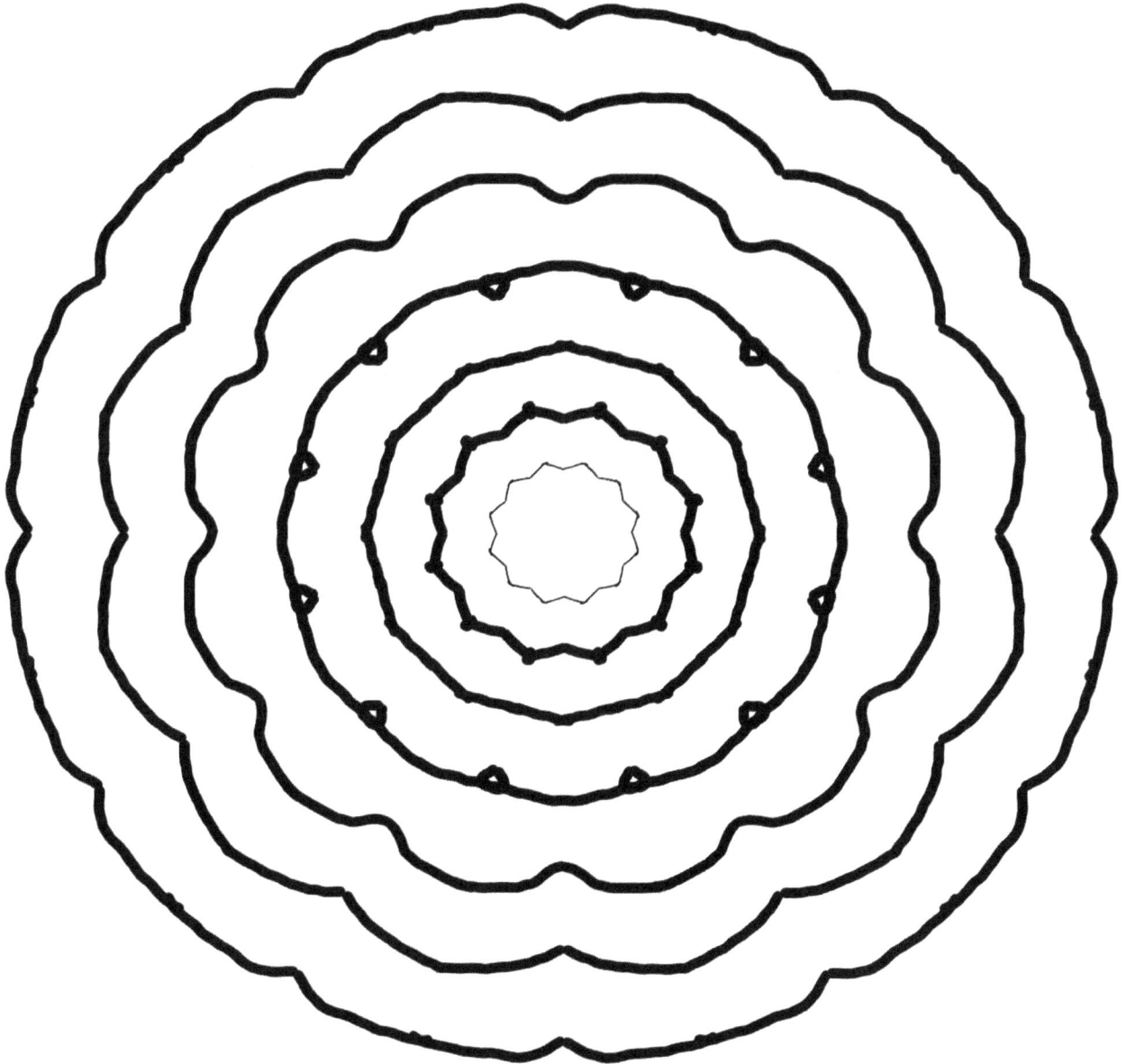

Add lines, shapes, and colors to this mandala so it expresses
your experience of happiness.

Bored

To feel like you don't care, or
don't want to do anything.

Fill this mandala with colors that express your experience
of boredom.

Bored

To feel like you don't care, or
don't want to do anything.

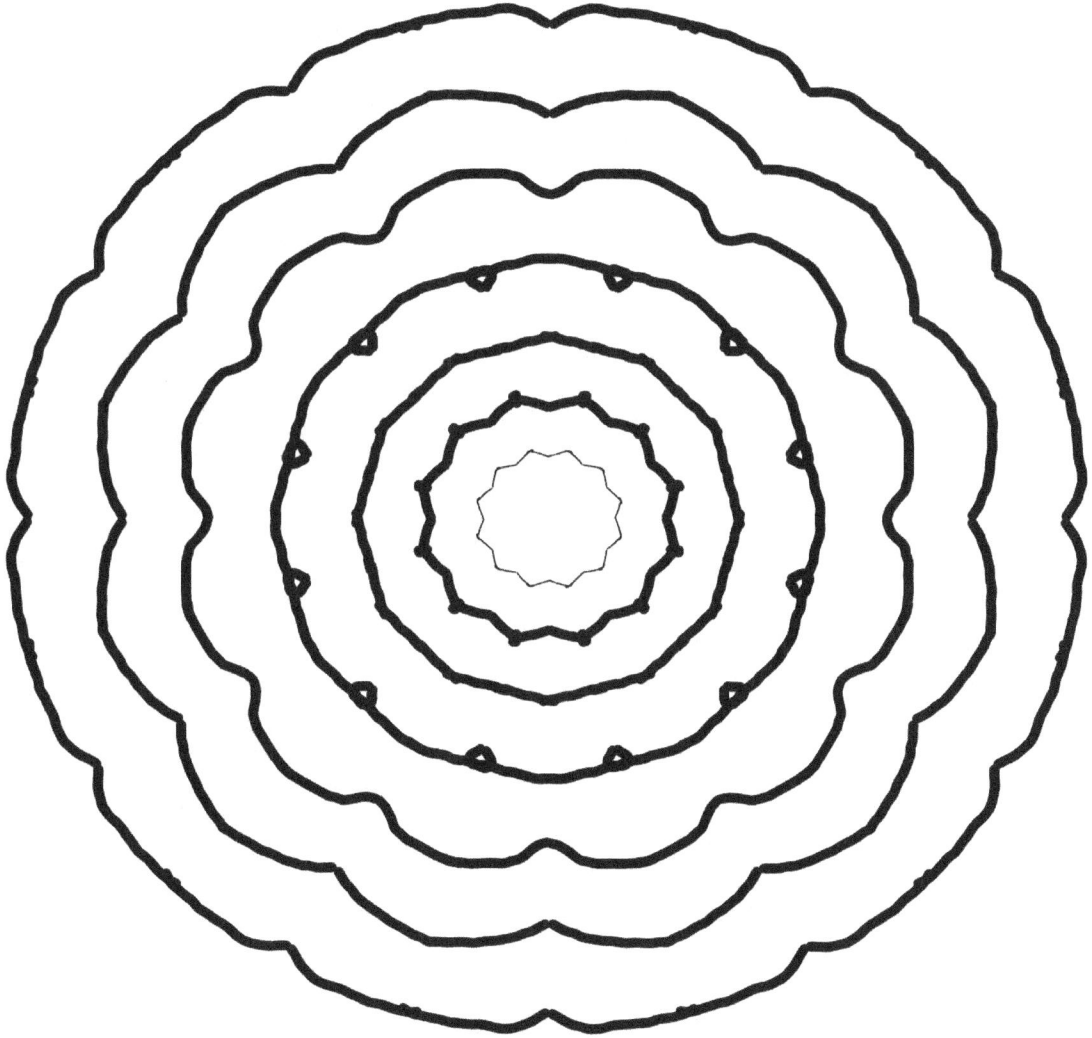

Add lines, shapes, and colors to this mandala so it
expresses your experience of boredom.

Hopeful

To feel like things are going to get better.

Fill this mandala with colors that express your experience of hope.

Hopeful

To feel like things are going to get better.

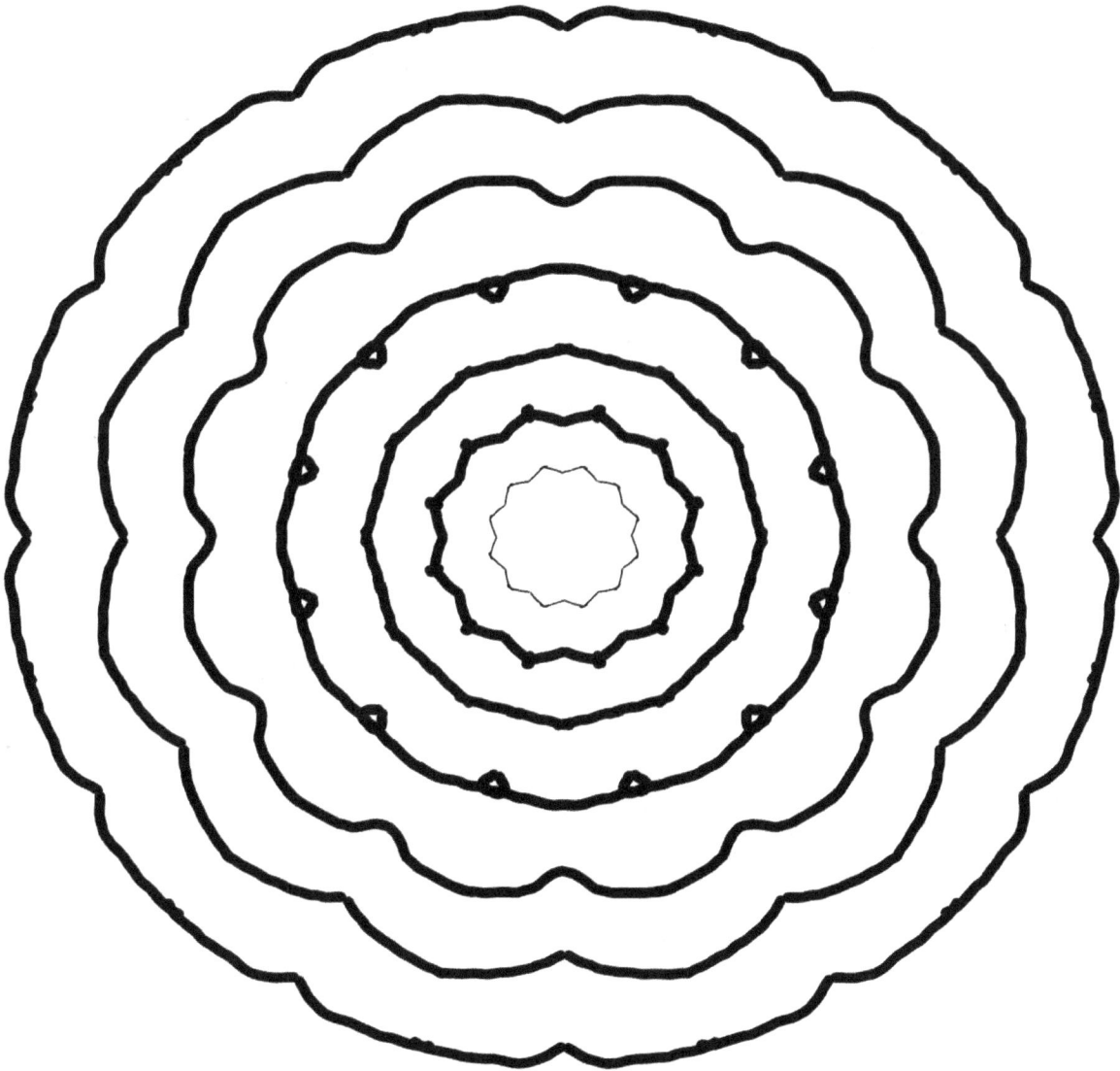

Add lines, shapes, and colors to this mandala
so it expresses your experience of hope.

Confused

To feel unsure about something.

Fill this mandala with colors that express your
experience of confusion.

Confused

To feel unsure about something.

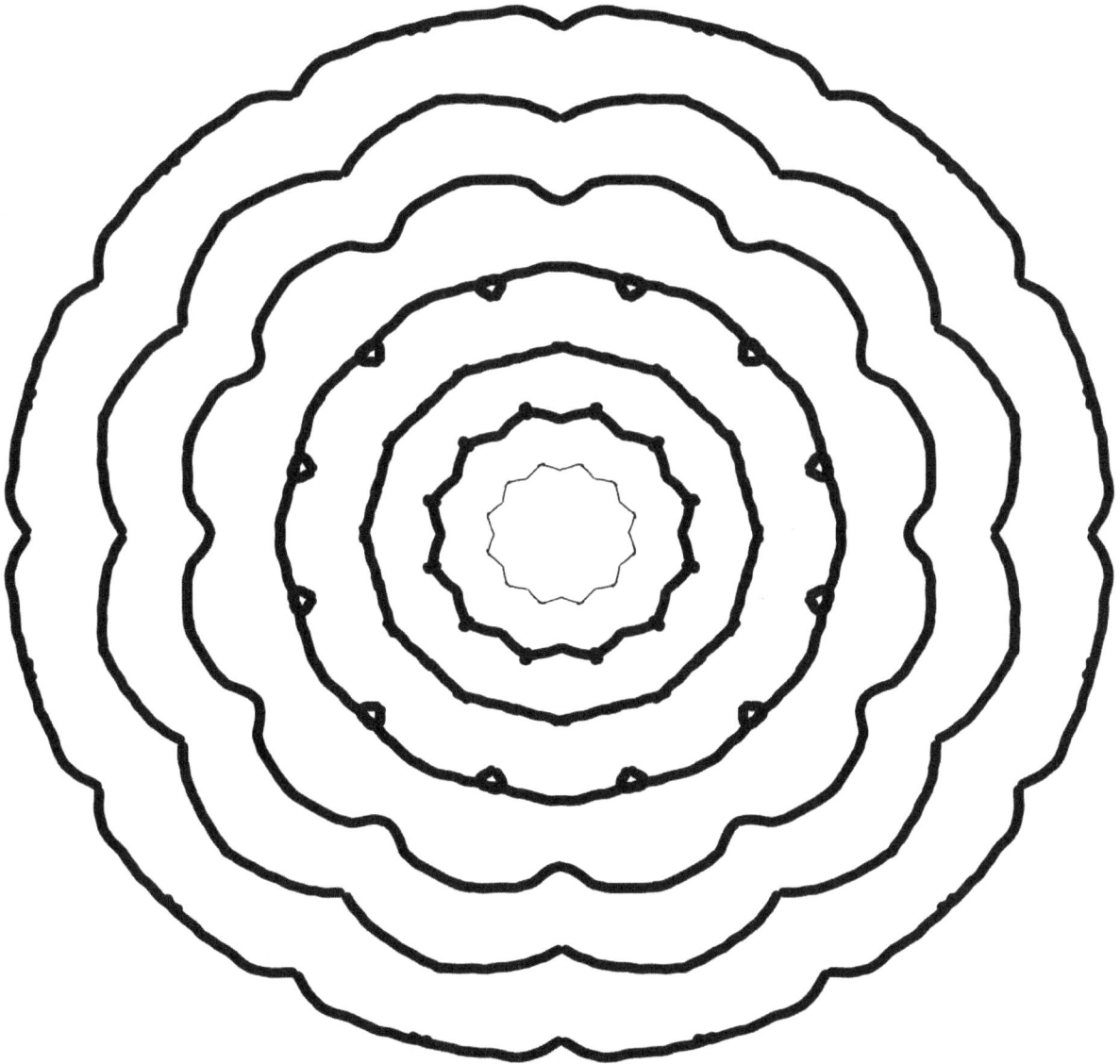

Add lines, shapes, and colors to this mandala
so it expresses your experience of confusion.

Disappointed

To feel like you cannot get what you want.

Fill this mandala with colors that express your
experience of disappointment.

Disappointed

To feel like you cannot get what you want.

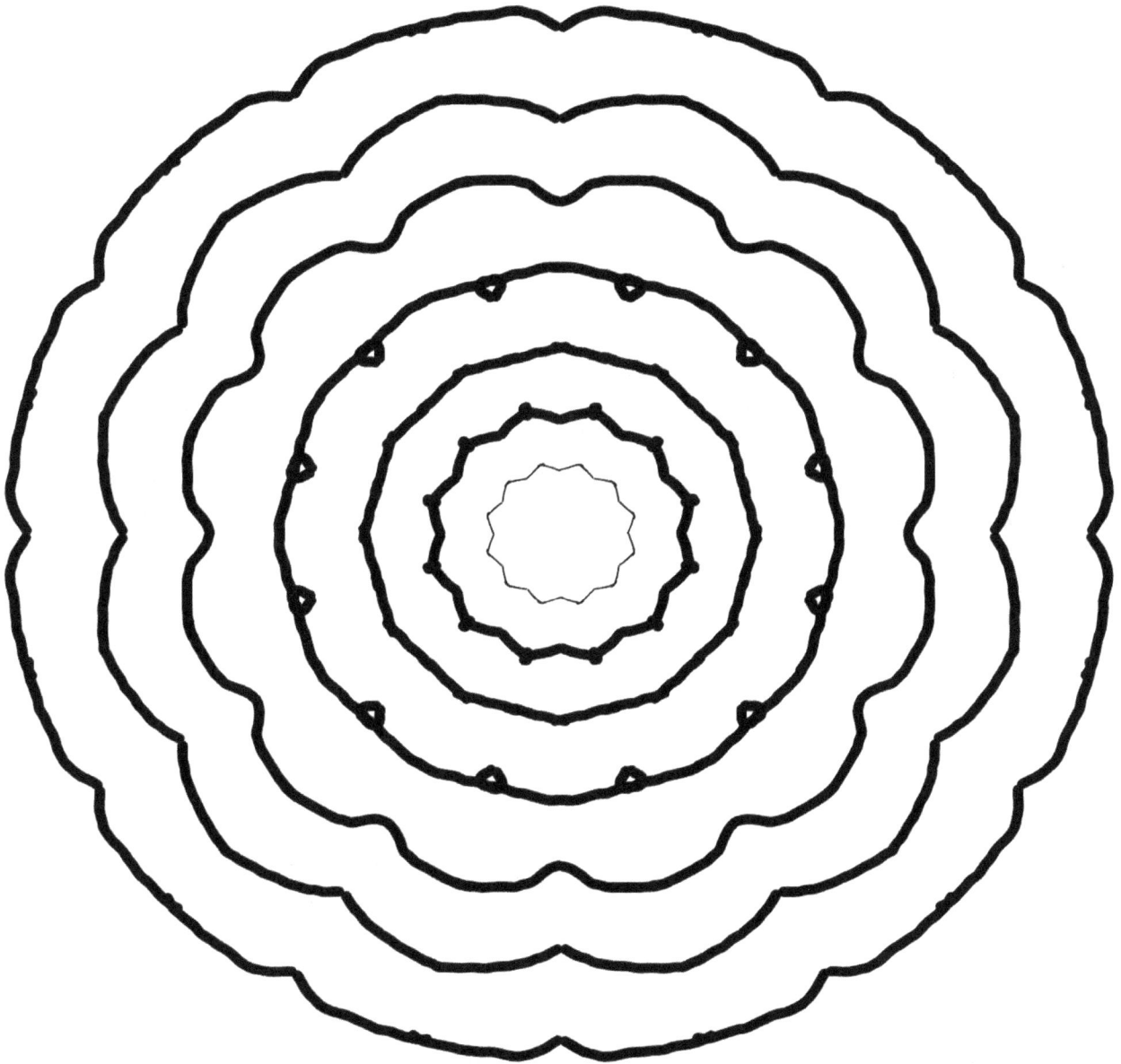

Add lines, shapes, and colors to this mandala so it
expresses your experience of disappointment.

Embarrassed

To feel ashamed.

Fill this mandala with colors that express your
experience of embarrassment.

Embarrassed

To feel ashamed.

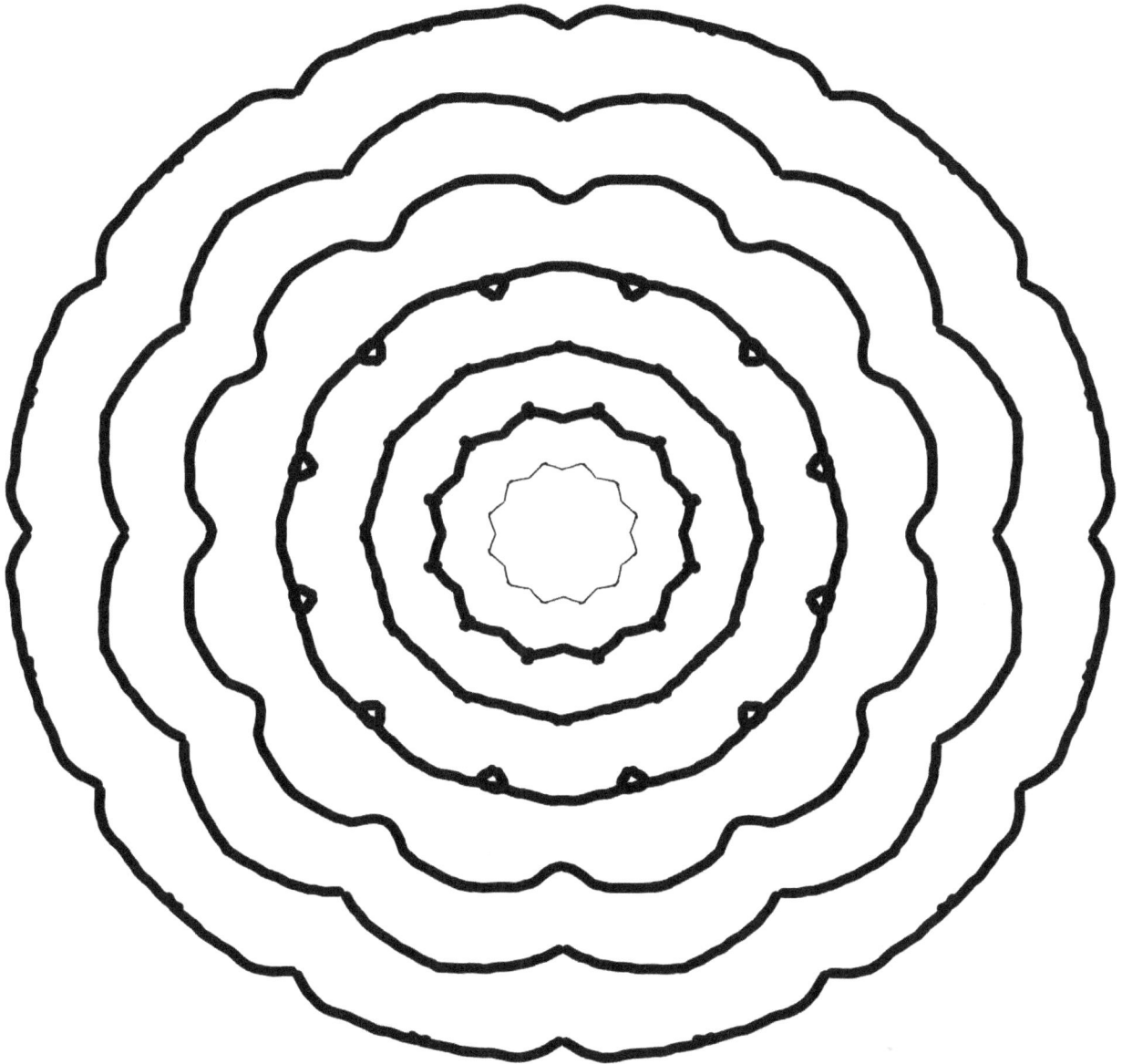

Add lines, shapes, and colors to this mandala so it expresses your experience of embarrassment.

Shy

To feel like you do not want others to notice you

Fill this mandala with colors that express your
experience of shyness.

Shy

To feel like you do not want others to notice you.

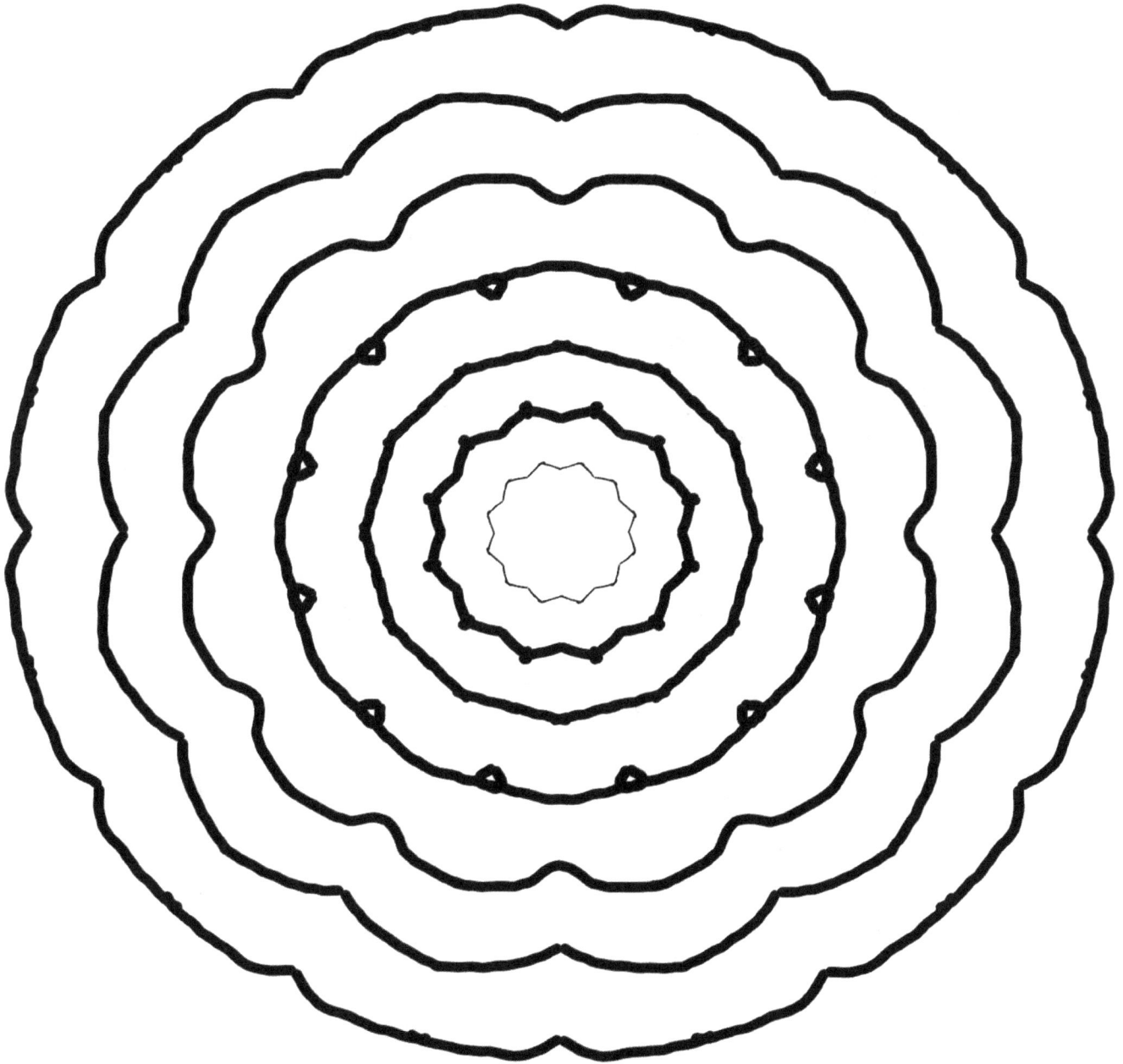

Add lines, shapes, and colors to this mandala so it
expresses your experience of shyness.

Frustrated

To feel stuck in a problem you cannot fix.

Fill this mandala with colors that express your
experience of frustration.

Frustrated

To feel stuck in a problem you cannot fix.

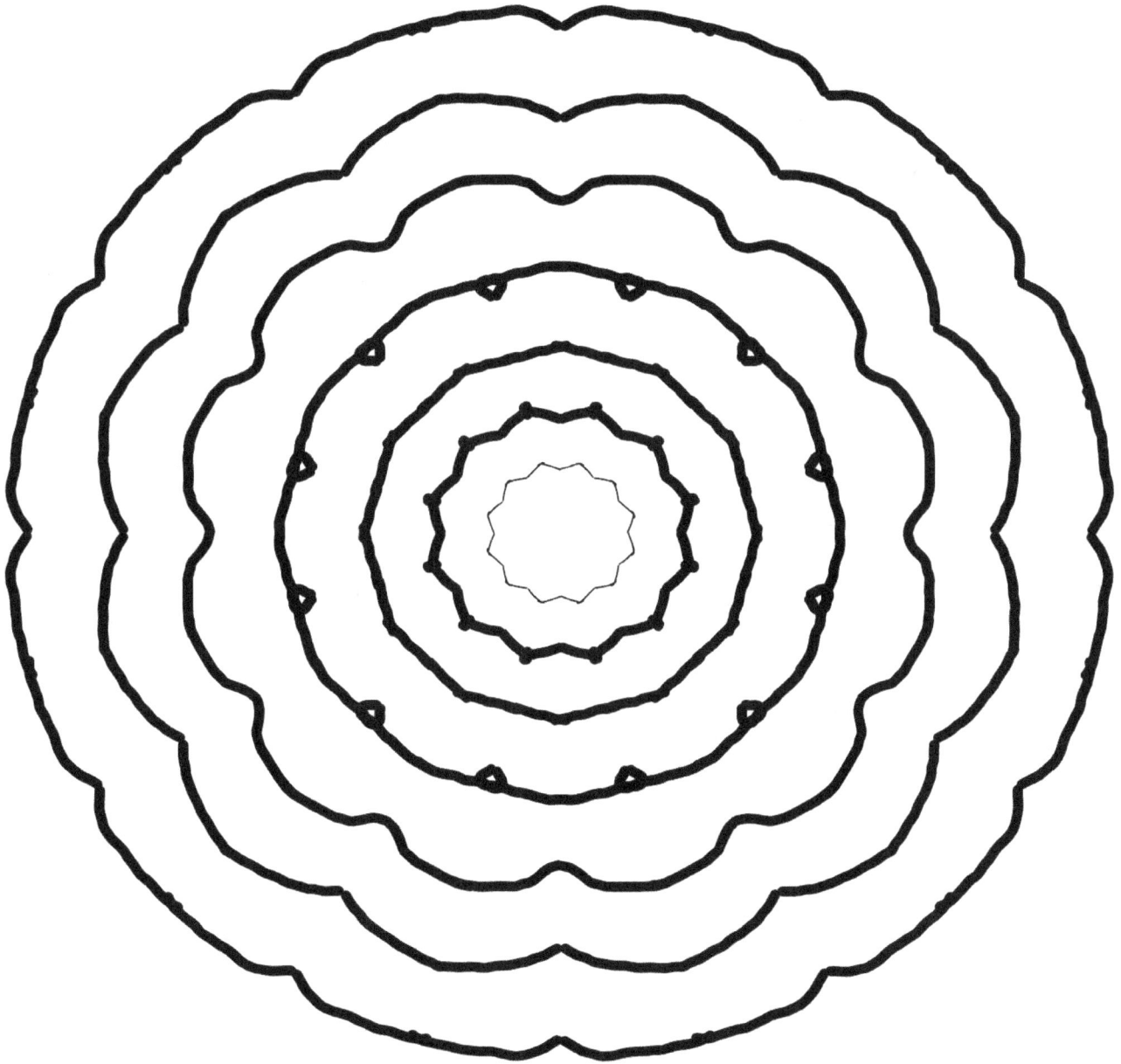

Add lines, shapes, and colors to this mandala so
it expresses your experience of frustration.

Grumpy

To feel bothered by others.

Fill this mandala with colors that express your experience of grumpiness.

Grumpy

To feel bothered by others.

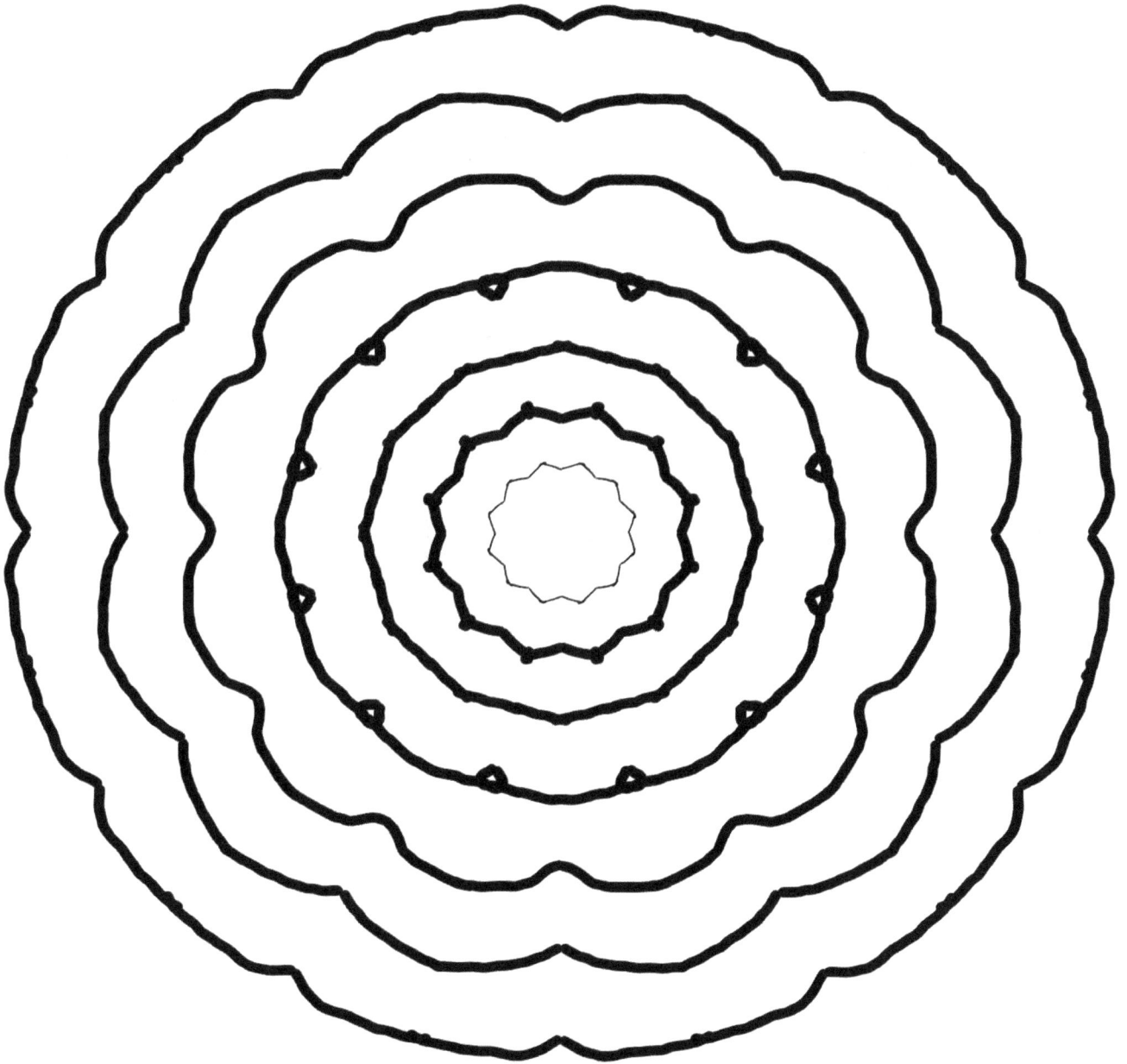

Add lines, shapes, and colors to this mandala so
it expresses your experience of grumpiness.

Guilty

To feel as if it is your fault.

Fill this mandala with colors that express your
experience of guilt.

Guilty

To feel as if it is our fault.

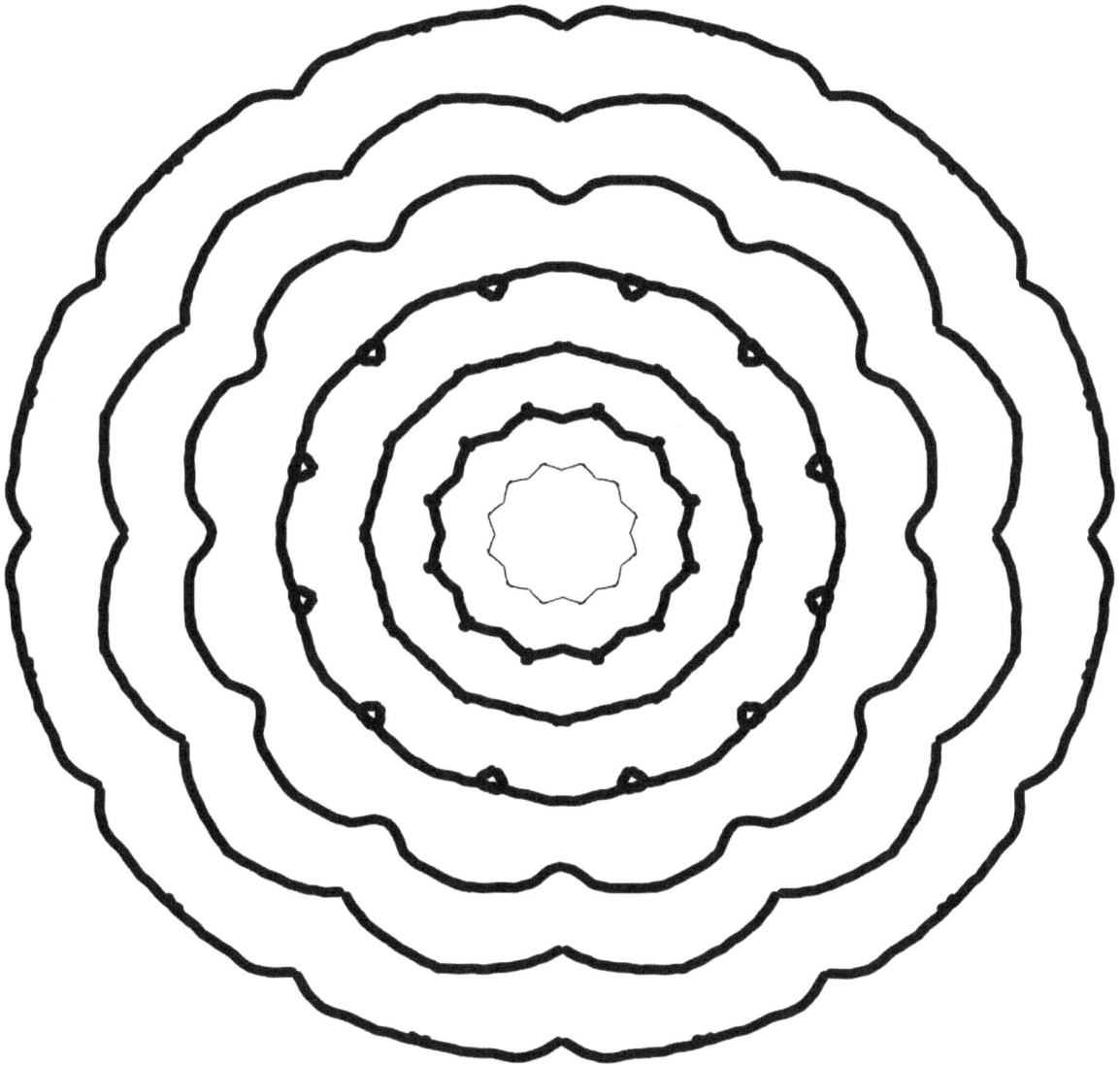

Add lines, shapes, and colors to this mandala so
it expresses your experience of guilt.

Sad

To feel loss, pain, and unhappiness.

Fill this mandala with colors that express your
experience of sadness.

Sad

To feel loss, pain, and unhappiness.

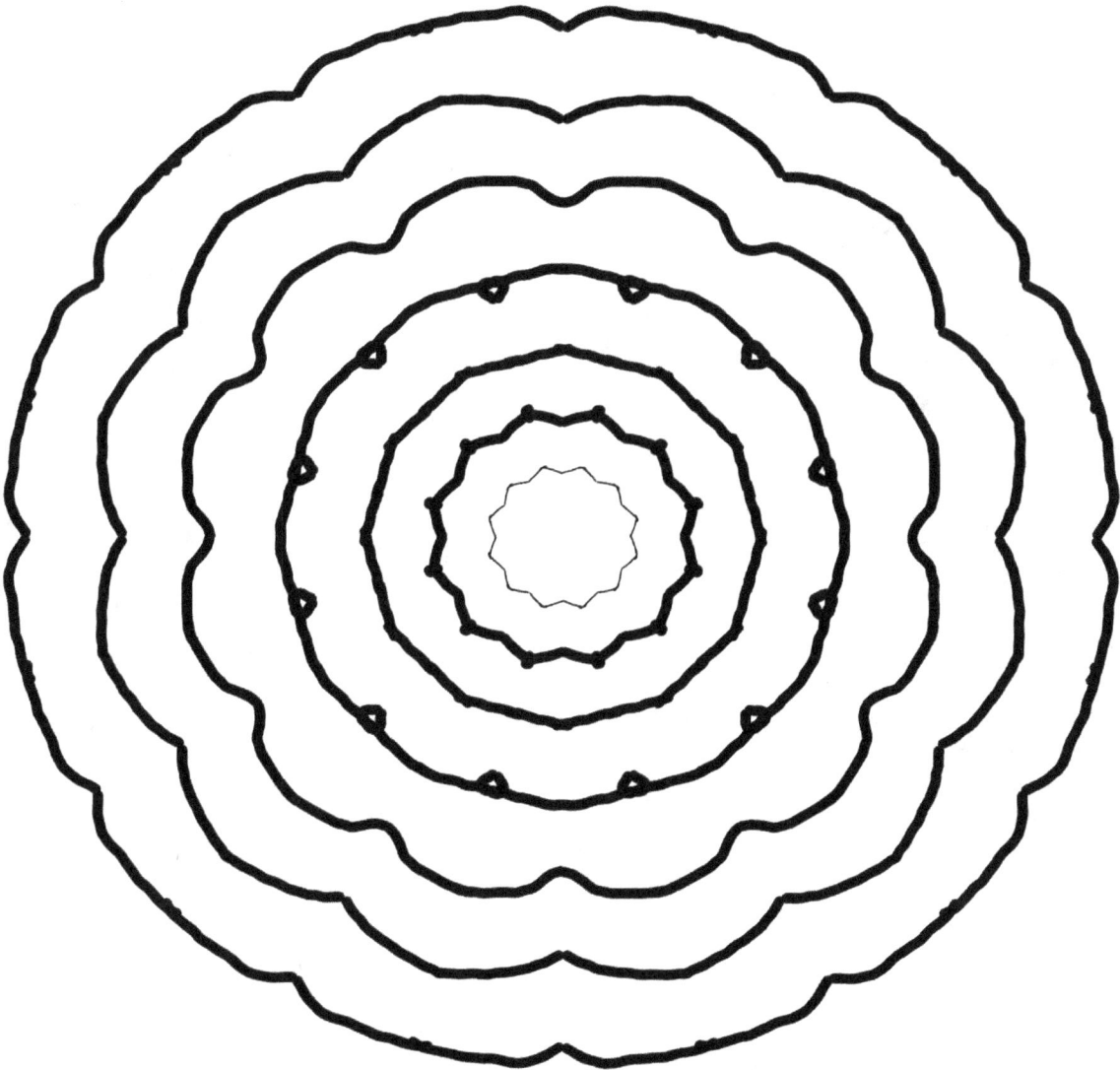

Add lines, shapes, and colors to this mandala so it
expresses your experience of sadness.

Hungry

To feel a need for food.

Fill this mandala with colors that express your experience of hunger.

Hungry

To feel a need for food.

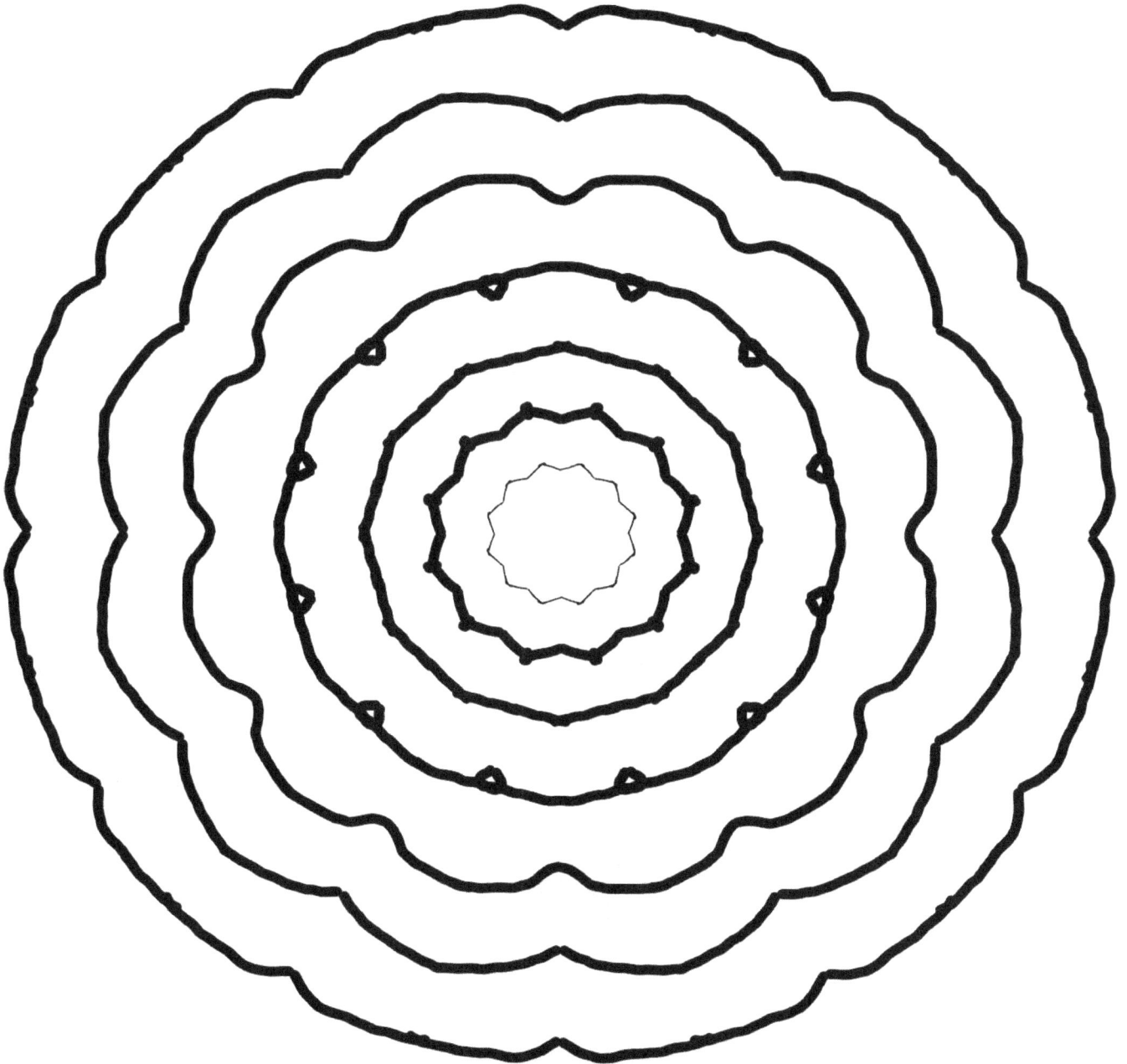

Add lines, shapes, and colors to this mandala so it
expresses your experience of hunger.

Sick

To feel ill like when your body hurts.

Fill this mandala with colors that express your experience of sickness.

Sick

To feel ill like when your body hurts.

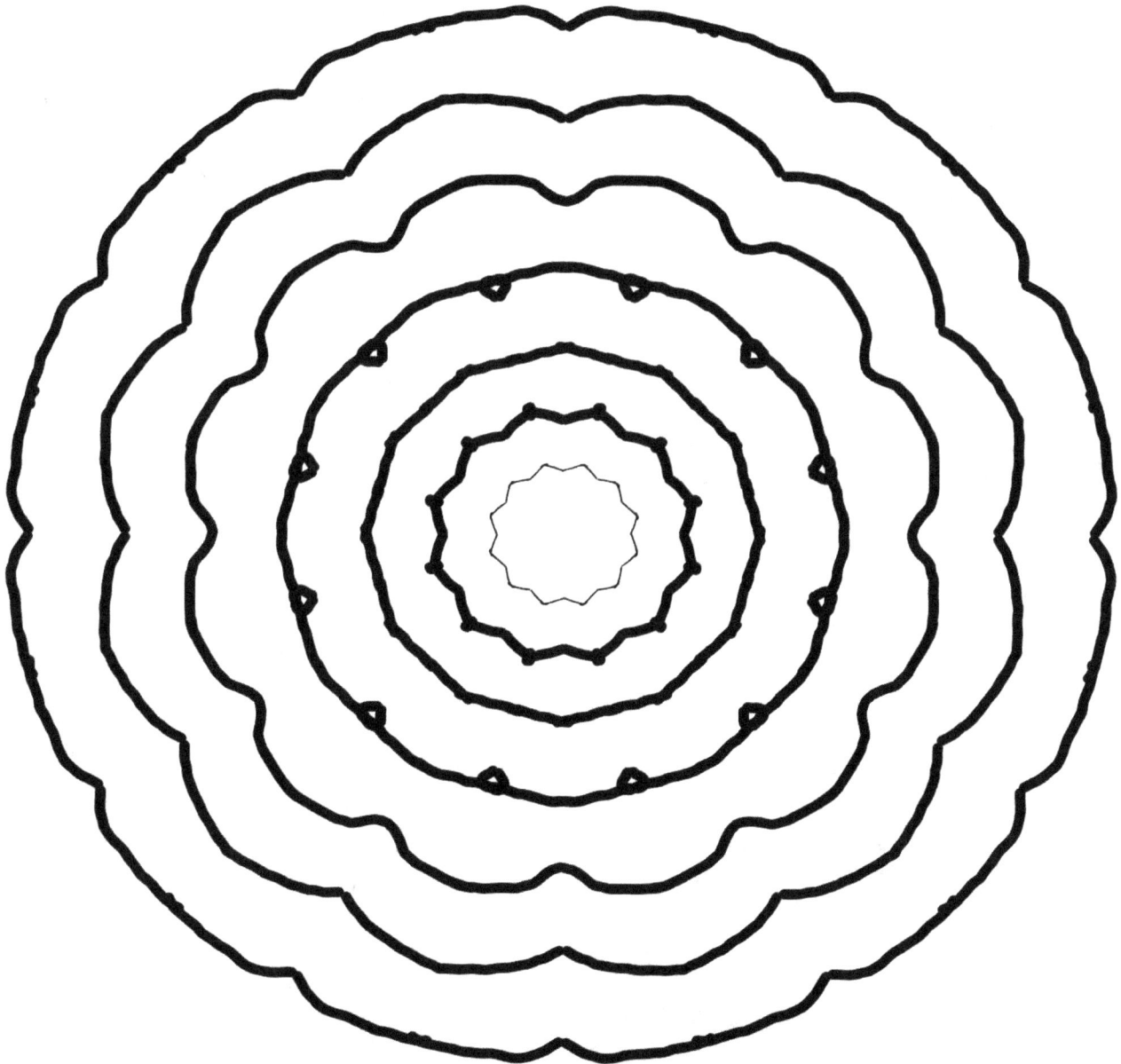

Add lines, shapes, and colors to this mandala so it
expresses your experience of sickness.

Worried

To feel afraid about what could go wrong.

Fill this mandala with colors that express your experience of worry.

Worried

To feel afraid about what could go wrong.

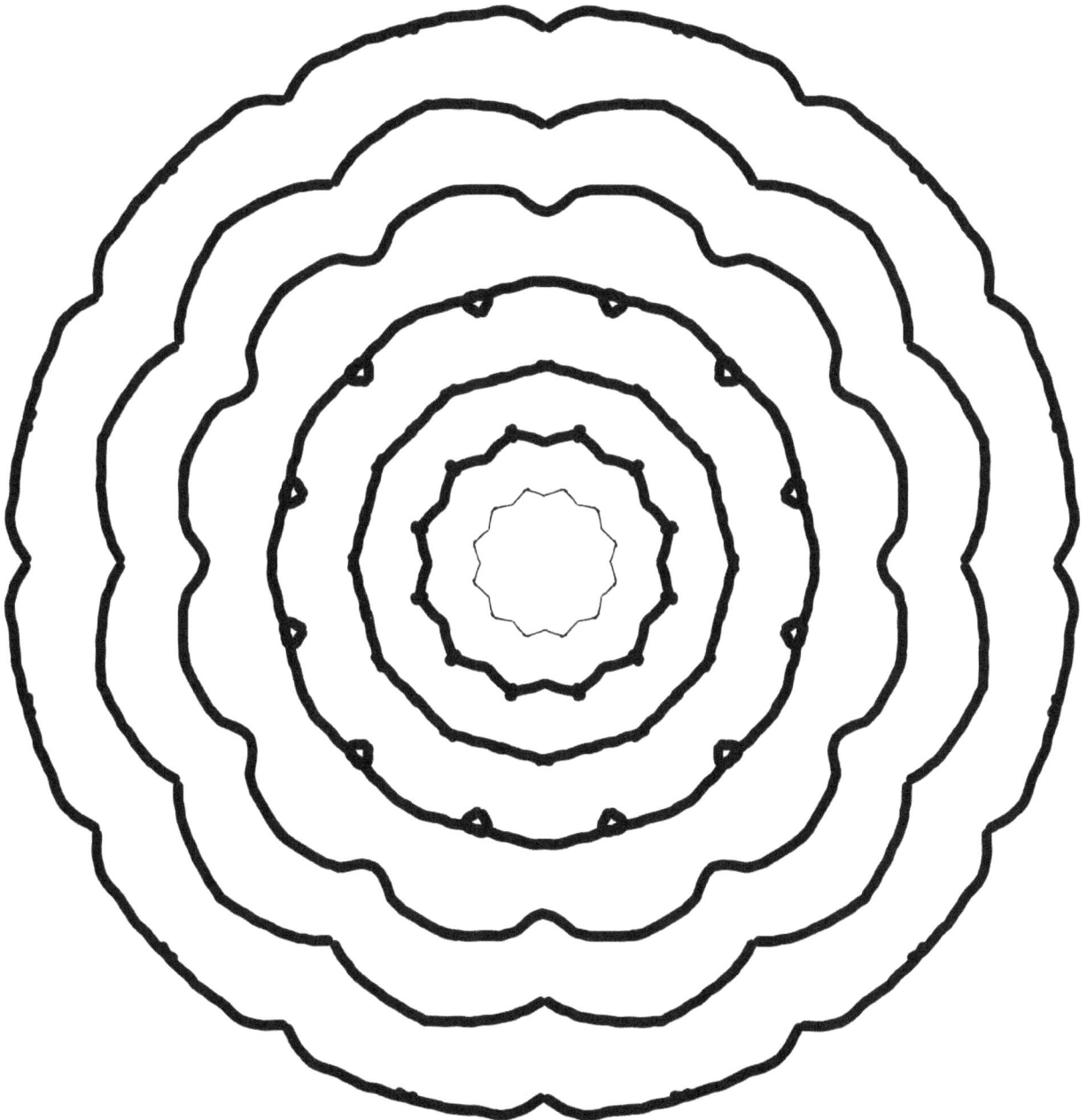

Add lines, shapes, and colors to this mandala
so it expresses your experience of worry.

Stressed
To feel bothered all the time.

Fill this mandala with colors that express your
experience of stress.

Stressed

To feel bothered all the time.

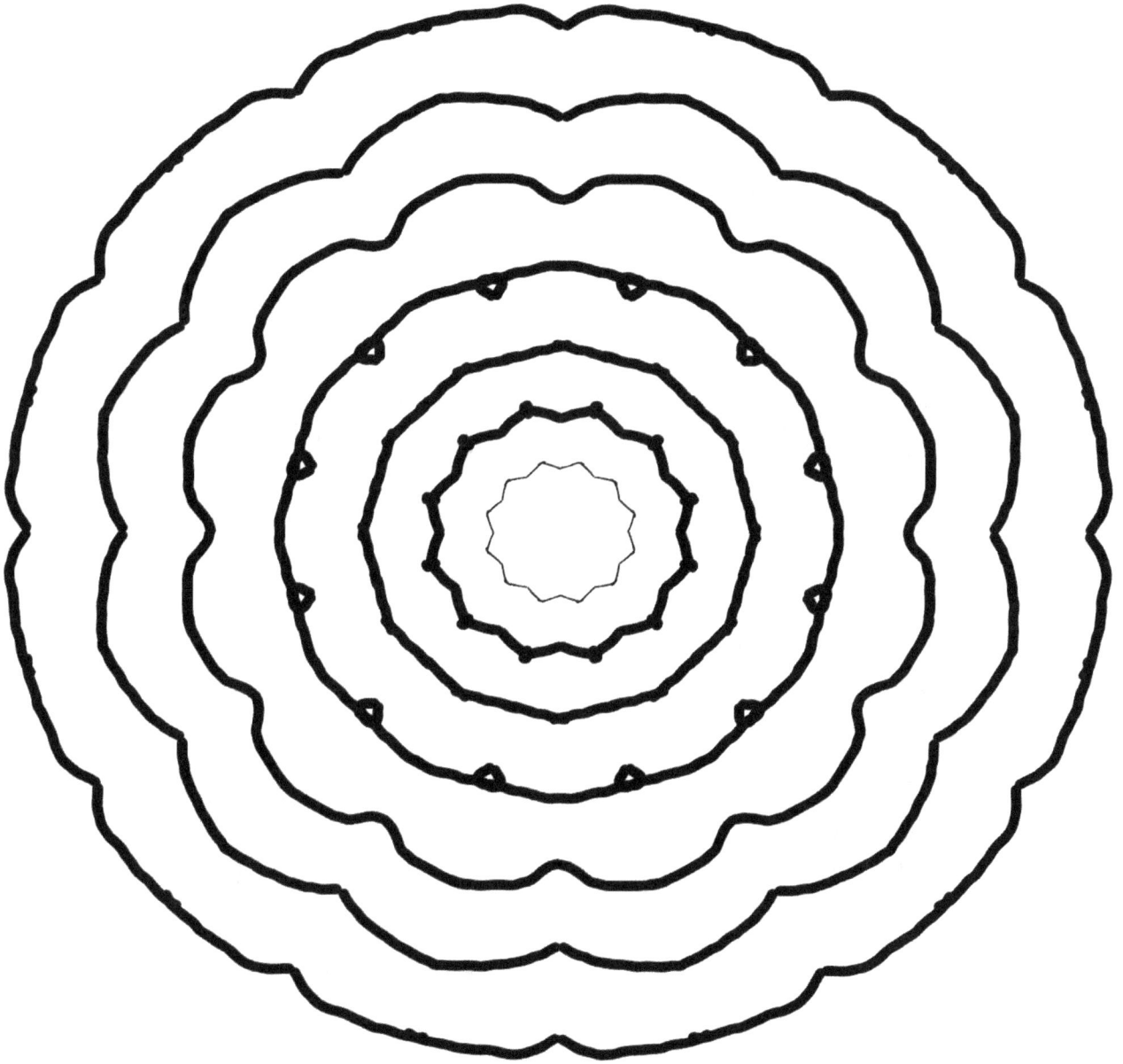

Add lines, shapes, and colors to this mandala so
it expresses your experience of stress.

Sleepy
To feel tired like you want to lay down.

Fill this mandala with colors that express your
experience of sleepiness.

Sleepy

To feel tired like you want to lay down.

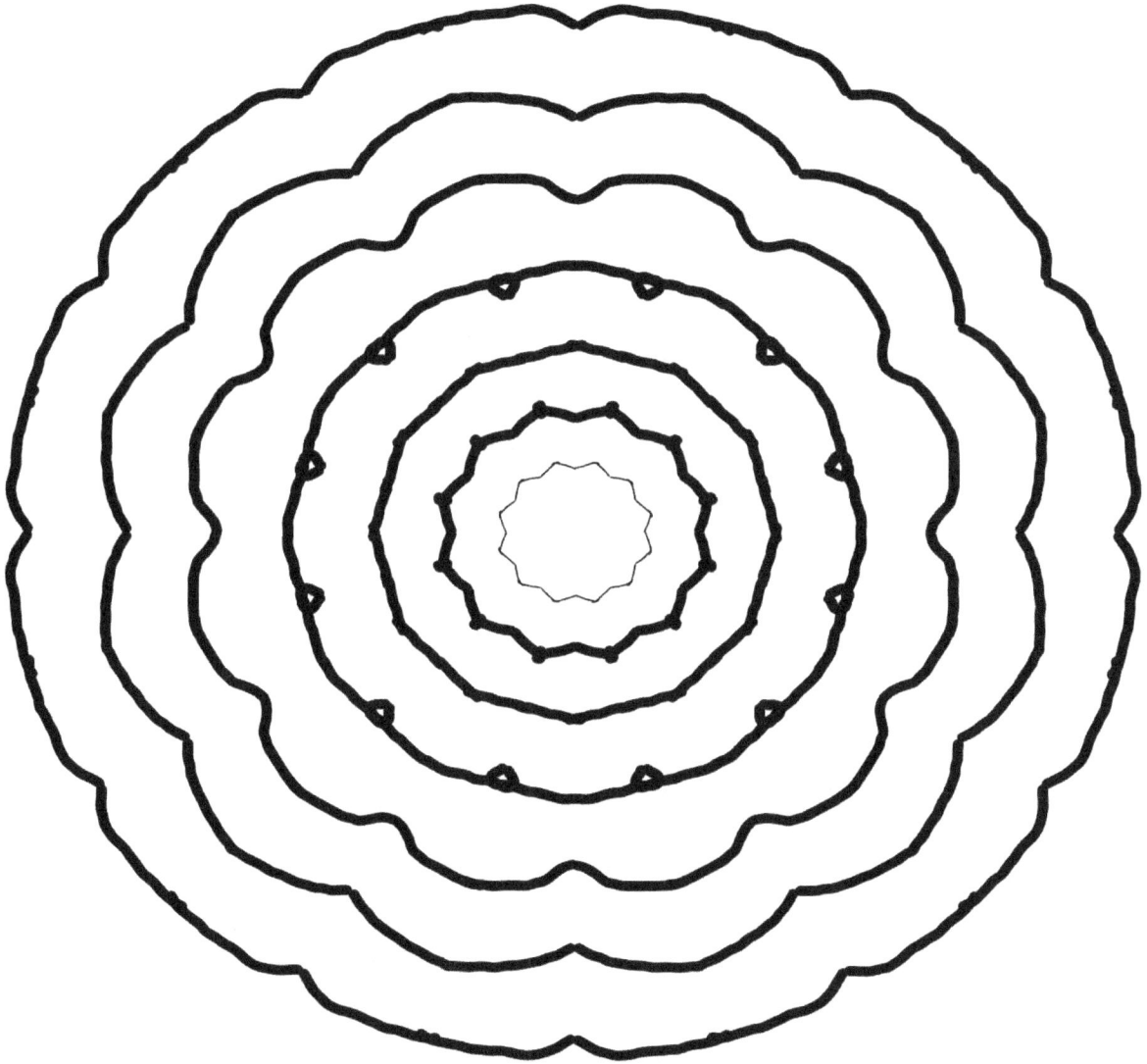

Add lines, shapes, and colors to this mandala so it expresses your experience of sleepiness.

What could this one be?

What feeling does this mandala express for you? Can you make it show the way you feel?

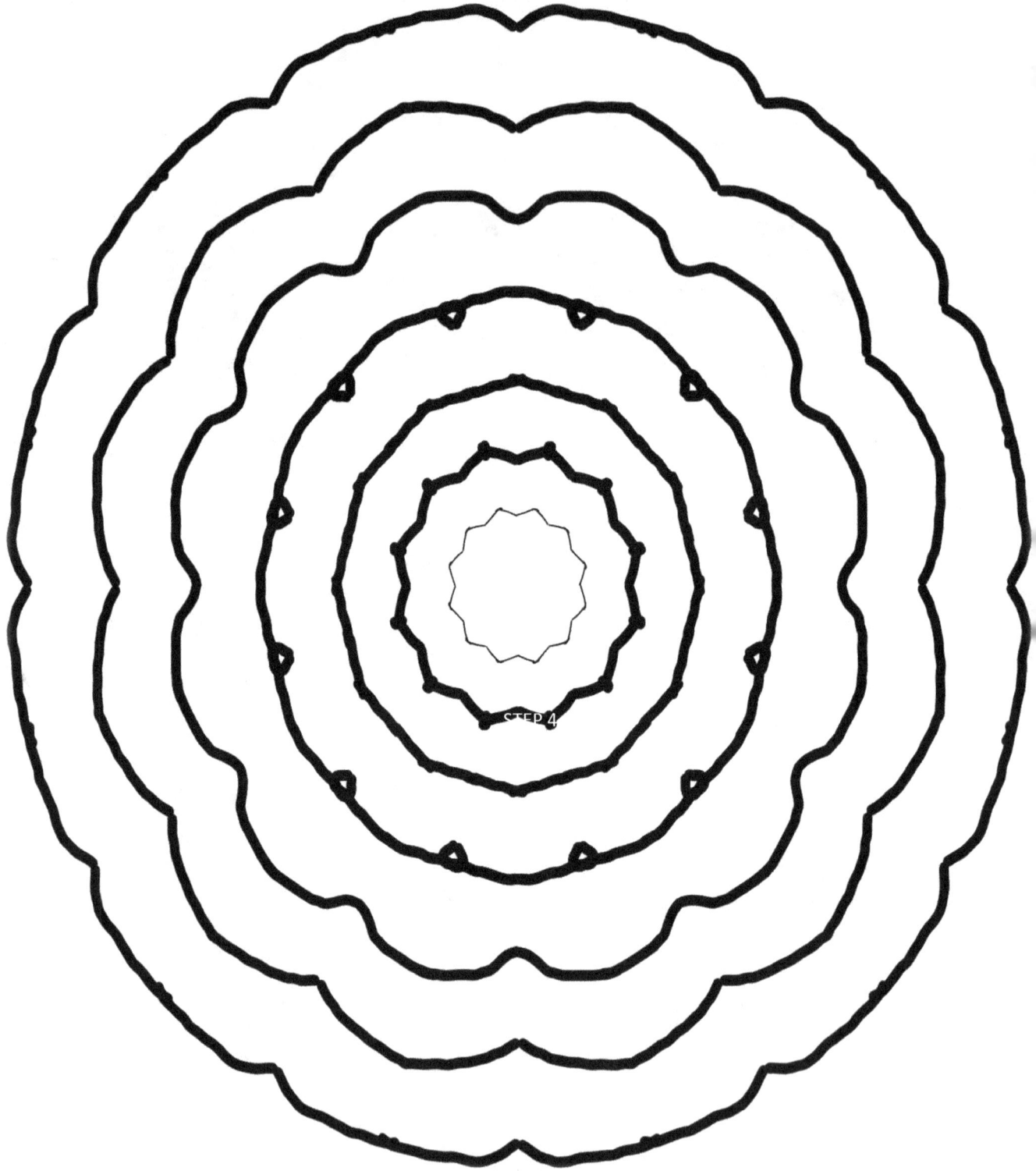

STEP 4

Draw, paint or color the feelings **_you_**

have inside?

ABOUT THE AUTHOR/ ILLUSTRATOR-

Karen White Porter is a Director of Loga Springs Academy and a Nationally Board-Certified Teacher. After graduating from Rutgers University with a Masters Degree in language education, she started teaching children. It was then that she realized the importance of emotional intelligence among her students. Having taught around the world gave her insight into to importance of the emotional underpinnings of how all people learn. She has taught at East China Normal University in Shanghai, P.R. China, Hofstra University in Hempstead N.Y., Hillside Public Schools in New Jersey, Saint Andrews University in Saint Andrews Scotland, Belcher Elementary in Clearwater Florida, The University of South Florida, The State University of Florida, and Loga Springs Academy.

ABOUT THE CO-AUTHOR

Dr. Martha Marcella Joseph Watts, affectionately called "Aunty Marcella", is an English teacher, teacher trainer, and an educational consultant.
She is best known for her Writing to Respond (WTR) process--an approach for guiding students in writing beyond summarizing, and for providing support to students for improving their performance in reading and writing. She has published several educational resources to support implementation of the WTR process. These resources include books, workbooks, classroom charts, student and educator wheels. The process, which has been in use in classrooms, schools, and a few districts since 2010, has helped schools and students realize 8-15 percentile gains over a three-semester period.

ABOUT THE BOOK-

Creating Emotion Mandalas guides us to connect with and sense our internal emotional reality—and to express our emotions through an art form born of ancient mystical traditions. It is a way to give visual shape to the ineffable within us. With mandalas we now can build easier access to experiences that are exceedingly difficult to define meaningfully.

Emotional Intelligence builds when we learn to observe and allow our emotions to be what they are or change if they need to without trying to force them to be or change to what we think they should be.

Unconscious cognitive and bodily methods we use to dim emotions down and cut them off from awareness cloud awareness, and experience of our feelings can fade through persistently looking at our inner life. Personal emotion mandalas gently bring awareness of emotional vocabulary. This can be the beginning of the expression of our emotions which will start to loosen up the stuck, repetitive, impulsive thinking and behavior that we have been using for so long to block our emotions. This loosening in turn allows a more natural flow of emotion, allowing more choice in behaving and thinking.

Paradigms depict the internal life of human beings as a flow of behaviors, thoughts, and feelings. Throughout the history of psychology, there has been disagreement about which causes the other, or whether external stimuli cause the rest.

Now, science recognizes that all three influence each other—reciprocally. Our feelings influence our thoughts, our thoughts influence our behaviors, our behaviors influence our feelings, our feelings influence our behaviors, our behaviors influence our thoughts, and our thoughts influence our feelings. And yes, external stimuli are part of the picture, too.

Many traditional methods only target behaviors or thoughts, perhaps because it seems easiest to define and work with them. However, we are rediscovering that direct access to our emotions is possible. They can be addressed directly. The key often lies in building a sensory connection to, and expression of, emotions.

Finally, and importantly, it is either a truth, or a particularly useful construct, to say that things go much deeper—that we have a soul. Mandalas bring us back to this deeper place—to the discovery of You.

Jim Porter, Ph.D., LMHC

www.ingramcontent.com/pod-product-compliance
Lightning Source LLC
Chambersburg PA
CBHW080946050426

42337CB00056B/4852